Sea Otters

Contents

What Are Sea Otters?

Sea otters are mammals.
They have warm blood.
They breathe air.

2

Did You Know?

Sea otters are sometimes called the *teddy bears of the sea.*

Sea otters have thick fur.
Their back paws have long, webbed toes.
They use their front paws like hands.

Webbed toes

Did You Know?

A sea otter holds its paws out of the water to keep them warm and dry.

Otters belong to the weasel family.
Badgers and skunks
belong to the weasel family, too.

River otter

Sea otter

Skunk

Badger

Weasel

7

Where Do Sea Otters Live?

Sea otters live in kelp forests
in the ocean.
They find food in the kelp.
They float on the kelp.

8

Did You Know?

Sea otters float in groups called rafts.

What Do Sea Otters Eat?

Sea otters eat sea urchins and abalone. They eat crabs, squid, fish, and clams. They need to eat a lot to keep warm.

Sea urchins

Kelp

Kelp

Did You Know?

Kelp is a type of seaweed. It grows very tall. Sea otters help the kelp forests by eating the sea urchins and abalone that eat the kelp.

Sea otters dive for their food.
They hold food with their front paws.
They take food to the surface to eat.
They lie on their backs when they eat.

Sea urchins

Did You Know?

A sea otter will sometimes use a stone to crack open shellfish.

After they have eaten, sea otters roll over and over in the water to wash away bits of food.

Otters rolling

14

They lick their fur and comb it with their claws.

Did You Know?

After sea otters have cleaned themselves, they blow air through their fur. This helps the sea otters keep warm.

Sea Otter Babies

Sea otter pups cannot swim
when they are born.
They sleep on their mother's chest.
Their mothers feed them milk.

When the mothers go looking for food, they wrap the pups in kelp to keep them safe.

Did You Know?

While the pup is lying on the mother's chest, the mother sinks down and lets the pup float. Soon the pup learns to swim.

Once the pups can swim,
they follow their mothers.
They learn how to find food.
The pups stay with their mothers
until they are two years old.

Did You Know?

Sometimes, in bad storms, pups get lost.

Sea Otters and People

Sometimes, if a sea otter's fur
gets covered with oil,
the sea otter can freeze to death.

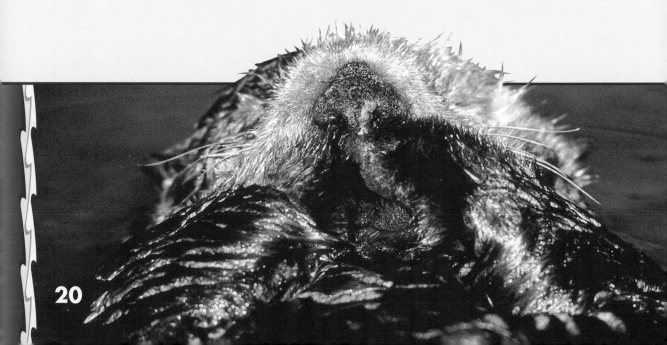

20

At the Monterey Bay Aquarium, human "sea otter moms" care for pups that are lost.

Feeding

Teaching

They teach the pups how to find food.

Diving

Releasing

At the Monterey Bay Aquarium, people can learn more about the *teddy bears of the sea.*

Index